Anonymous

**Rose Tremaine**

The Blackberries and Other Stories

Anonymous

**Rose Tremaine**
*The Blackberries and Other Stories*

ISBN/EAN: 9783744686198

Printed in Europe, USA, Canada, Australia, Japan

Cover: Foto ©Thomas Meinert / pixelio.de

More available books at **www.hansebooks.com**

# ROSE TREMAINE,

## OR

## THE BLACKBERRIES,

### AND

## OTHER STORIES.

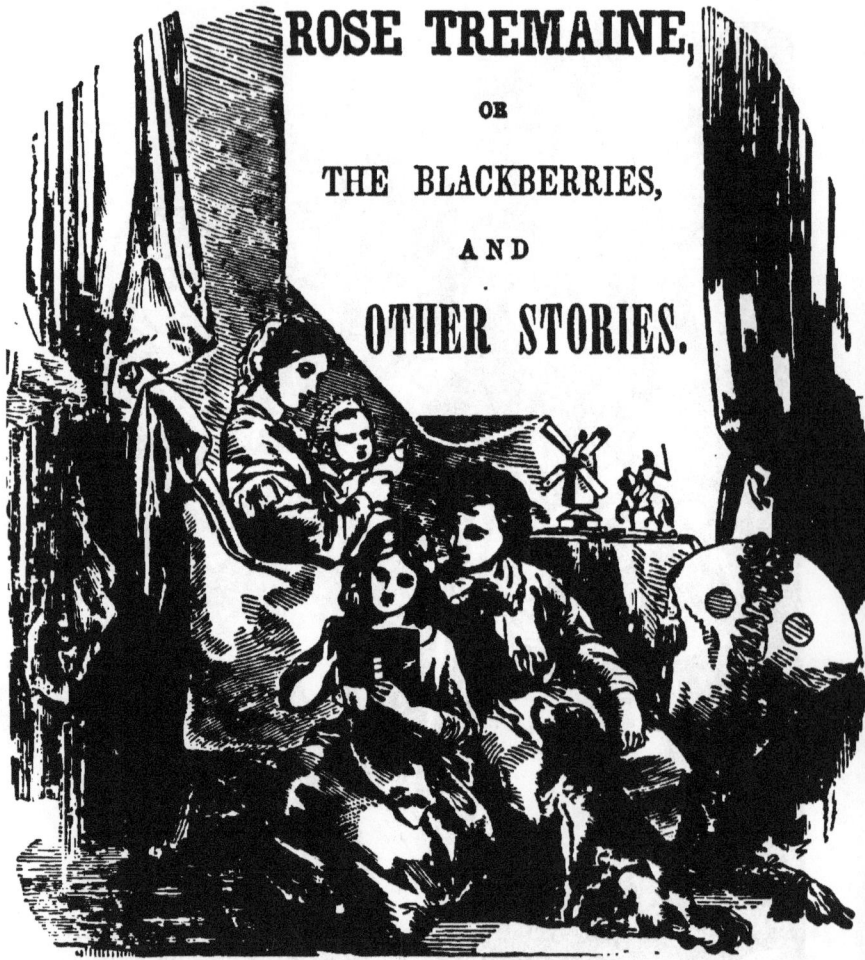

BOSTON:

CROSBY & AINSWORTH.

NEW YORK: OLIVER S. FELT.

1866.

# STORIES.

## THE BLACKBERRIES.

In Cumberland there are, as everybody knows, a number of beautiful lakes; some are large, and others small, but most of them have pretty little woody islands dotted over their surface, and fairy bays and headlands on their shores. In the numerous peaceful valleys which slope from the lofty hills to the water's edge, are built pretty villages and hamlets, and many handsome houses are

(5)

scattered about in the woods, and on the promontories above them.

In one of these vales was a village more secluded than ordinary from the world's notice. Its inhabitants were chiefly composed of farmers, and the laborers whom they employed. Among the latter, there was nowhere to be found a more industrious and clever, or more cheerful man, than Édward Trevaine; he was always in request wherever work requiring more than usual talent and knowledge was to be done, and consequently he gained more money than most of his companions; this might have made them jealous, had he not been ever ready to help them in sorrow or want to the best of his ability. Trevaine was also blessed by the possession of a good wife, and one sweet little daughter, who was the pride and delight, not only of her parents, but of the whole village. Mothers told their children to follow the example of little Rose, and fathers said how happy the Tremaines must be in her good conduct. At school her lessons were ready first, and repeated the most perfectly; at play she was always kind and obliging, and never quarrelsome; and at home she was obedient and affectionate; never giving trouble, but watching for opportunities to assist her kind mother in her household work; but still Rose was not perfectly good; she used sometimes, though very seldom, to do what she was

not told to do; and I will give you an
account of one of these sad occasions.

Rose returned from school one bright
morning, in the beginning of autumn,
with her neat little book-bag on her arm,
and her sweet face beaming with happiness. She ran across the well-stocked
garden, and entering the cottage threw
her arms round her mother's neck, and
kissed her.

"Have you been good this morning,
darling?" was the kind question with
which she was greeted.

"Yes, mother! and now I want you
to grant me a favor! Will you?"

"What is it dear?"

"May I go into the field above the
sand bay, to see if the blackberries are

ripe? I won't eat many, but will bring them home to you, my own dear mother; and if I get a great quantity you will make a pudding for Sunday, and father will be so pleased!"

"Yes," replied her mother, "you may go dear; but mind you do not go beyond the first field, or I shall not know where to find you for dinner."

So Rose put her books in the cupboard, and, after promising obedience, took her little basket and bounded from the house. She soon reached the desired spot, and hunted all over the hedges and brambles she could find, but there was no ripe fruit on them; and she picked a few flowers, wandered on towards the stile that led into the next field; this was quickly reached, and Rose looked over it. She stretched out her head to see if any blackberries were ripe there, and perceived, not within reach of where she stood, but yet so near, that if she only just got over the gate she could obtain them, a large bunch of the finest she had seen that day.

"Oh," thought Rose, "I must have these; I will only cross the stile and come back again. Mother's reason for telling me not to go, was in case she should not be able to find me." And in one moment she had disobeyed, and was standing on the other side of the hedge, eagerly plucking the berries. When they were gathered, Rose looked further, and at about half a dozen yards' distance

were a great many more, so she said to
herself,—"Well, just these, and I will
go back;" but when these were also de-
posited in her basket, she was tempted
afresh, and I am sorry to say, strayed
from bramble to bramble, till she had
reached the opposite stile that led into a
third field; here she again peeped, and a
bunch of nuts tempted her to transgress
still further, and the little girl yielded,
and went after them. She picked the
nuts from the tree, and looked around
her; the hedge was formed of nut trees
and brambles, and she thought, that as
she had gone into the enclosure, she
might as well get all she could; and she
walked on, pulling every nut or berry
that she saw. By and by she reached a

part of a fence which joined a wild wood, that covered the sides and summit of one of the highest hills on the borders of the lake; just before her was a gap that had been made by the village children, when on nutting excursions, and inside the edge of the forest was a beautiful bed of wild strawberries.

"Oh!" exclaimed the little girl, "how beautiful they look! I will pick them, and then I must run back as fast as I can." So she scrambled through the hedge, and began to gather the fruit in great haste; but the bank was a long one, and led some way into the wood; besides, the nuts hung in clusters around, and Rose was tempted on, till at last she lost the path.

There were a great many little roads through the wood, and she ran about looking and longing for the one that led to the village, but she could not find it. Then she called to her mother as loud as she could, but her mother could neither hear nor answer her; so at last she sat down on the mossy-root of a large oak tree, and cried very bitterly. "Oh dear!" she said, "how unhappy am I! What will become of me? I shall never find my way out of the wood, and the gipsies will take me away." And her tears flowed afresh. But soon Rose felt hungry; she had not eaten since her breakfast, and it was now far advanced in the afternoon; so she took the wild fruits that had seduced her into the wood, and made an unsubstantial meal of them. After resting a little she again set out on her wanderings; but turn where she would the paths only led further into the forest. Poor Rose now began to be very frightened and very sad, and she wished she had staid in the first field and done as her mother had bidden her.

She walked a long way further, and saw that the sun was getting very low, and then she stood still by the side of a little spring of water that welled up from beneath a bit of gray rock, thickly covered with yellow lichen, and over which the bare and knotty roots of the trees were hanging. Rose waited and watched till the sun was gone, and darkness had spread its mantle over the quiet earth.

She did not heed the little birds that were twittering "Good night" to one another in the branches, or the merry chirp of the grasshoppers come out for their evening stroll; but she thought of her dear mother, and her little heart was bursting with its load of grief and guilt. It was useless to go further, and Rose's feet were swollen already with walking; so she sat down by the gray stone and gazed on the tiny pool formed by the crystal spring. As she watched it she saw the reflected image of a star trembling on its mirror-like surface, and Rose raised her weeping eyes to the blue heaven above. There she saw the countless lamps of light burning in their glory; and as her thoughts reverted to the God who had created them, she bent her knees and fervently supplicated mercy and protection. She rose calm and comforted, and then laid herself down on the green moss and grass to rest before she again attempted to reach the village.

Meantime all was grief and sorrow in the hamlet. Mrs. Trevaine went to call Rose, and found she was not in the first field; she searched for her in those adjoining, but in vain. She then flew back to the village, and asked her neighbors if they had seen her lost child. But all said "No:" and the terrified mother became frantic with anxiety. Her husband now returned from his work with the other men, and on hearing the sorrowful

tale, they all agreed to go in quest of the
the little truant.

Accordingly, they formed into numerous parties, and took different routes,
agreeing to return to the village by an
appointed hour, so that if none of them
had found Rose they might consult about
further plans of search. The time so
anxiously looked for by the agonised
mother at length arrived, and the men
were discovered approaching on their return. The children ran towards them to
learn news of their lost companion, but
did not hasten back to their mothers, for
they had no joyful tidings to communi-
cate. In a few minutes the various parties had met on the village green, under
the branches of the aged lime tree; and,

2

after comparing their adventures, and echoing the tale of disappointment from mouth to mouth, Edward and a few of the kindest of his neighbors arranged to make one more trial that night in the wood, and armed with stout sticks and lanterns they set out, accompanied by the prayers of all who remained behind. After wandering and searching for some time, without obtaining so much even as a trace of the lost child, one of the men, who was separated some distance from the rest, hailed them with the cry of "Found, found!" All hurried to the sound of the voice, and there, lying on the green moss, was little Rose in a troubled sleep. Her father caught her in his arms, and, with a loud scream, tho little creature recognized him in the uncertain light, and buried her burning face on his shoulder. Questions were rapidly put to the poor child, and answered by her with shame and sorrow and the men prepared to carry her back to the village in triumph. Rose, in the meantime, told her father that she was dreaming at the very moment he awoke her that a wolf was eating her up, and said she was trying to pray to God to save her from it. In the course of an hour they were descried from the village green, and this time the little folks who flew to meet them vied with each other in trying who should first reach the anxious group of men and women, and tell them that dear Rose was safe. The pastor, who was occupied in his study, came out to meet them, and after the first delirium of joy was over, he called upon his flock to return thanks to God for the preservation of the beloved child. What words can picture the beauty of the scene which followed? There, on the soft grass under the old tree, knelt many an aged man and woman, many a hale, hearty laborer and his wife, and many a light-hearted child. All were hushed in solemn silence, while their venerated minister, with Rose kneeling beside him, implored the pardon of God for her fault, and His blessing upon her, and that His watchful eye might be over every one then before Him, to protect them from all evil and save them from sin. He then called on the assembly to sing a hymn of praise, and afterwards dismissed them with his blessing. The benighted traveller started on his road to hear the notes of thanksgiving swelling on the moonlit air, and paused and hung on the notes till they died away, when, with a full heart and chastening sigh, he resumed his way, wondering whence those voices could have arisen, so sweet, so full of meaning were the souls who sung.

# THE WAX DOLL.

OFTEN when a little girl, have I stood at shop-windows, gazing at wax dolls. They seemed far beyond my reach, for I had no money to purchase them. And yet they looked so smiling, it was hard to leave them and go home to my alabaster doll, Sally, whose beauty had long since departed.

Sometimes carriages would before the shop-doors where I was peeping in, bearing richly dressed ladies, and little girls, looking as fine as the wax dolls. Then the steps were let down with a great slam, and they tripping along entered the shop. They asked for wax dolls, and I must needs look on to see which was the chosen one. A little girl would hold it forth so pleased, that I had to be pleased too as she rustled by me in her silk dress and sprang into the carriage, not even knowing that I was standing near. But as she passed, I could hear her mama say anxiously, sometimes,—

"Take care, my daughter, do not hurt your new doll."

I went home and was soon consoled by my alabaster baby, Sally, which I held without fear.

Once I went to visit a little girl, who had a splendid wax doll sent to her from her uncle in London. But where do you think it was? It was in a glass case. I was allowed to look at its red cheeks, and curling hair, and satin slippers, and gay sash, but not to touch her. A very careful, big person, could take her out of the case, and pull a wire that opened and shut her eyes, but no child was allowed to pull that mysterious wire. What great wonder took hold of my mind when I saw those eyes close and open! But I went home to my plain doll Sally more satisfied than ever. I kissed her and tossed her in the air, and when she came down head first, I laughed, and said,

"It is better to have you, Sally, though you are not so pretty, than a wax doll in a case!

Since I became a woman I have seen

many wax dolls,—gay, happy-looking things. Some were new-year's gifts; some, birth-day presents; and the little children to whom they were presented seemed gay and happy too: but once I saw a wax doll in a coffin, and I will tell you how it was.

I knew a little boy whom I shall call Angel, because he is now an angel in heaven. He was like a beautiful doll when he was alive, for he had large blue eyes, and light curling hair, and a round, smooth face, and a dimpled smile.

This little boy had a friend about three years old. I will call her Cherub, because she, too, is now a cherub in heaven. She did not look like a doll; her features were not so regular as the boy's, but there was something wonderfully sweet in her darkly bright eyes, that made you think of light and love, and then she sang like one of Heaven's children before her time.

Well, Angel was taken ill, and after a few days of suffering he said,—

"Mama, I wish you to get my own money, that is in my little purse, and buy a wax doll for Cherub."

His mama said—"Yes, my child;" but before she could keep her promise he went to sleep in Christ, or as some say, he died.

Then his mama, weeping that her child was gone, yet glad that he was free from pain and tears, remembered her promise. So she went to Angel's own little purse, and took out the money and bought a wax doll, and sent it to Cherub, saying, that an angel had given it to her.

Cherub took the doll in her arms, and sang sweet songs to it, and talked about Angel, and began to think of heaven.

Soon after Cherub became ill of the same disease that took away Angel. She often asked for her doll, and while she had breath, sang, with her clear, rich voice, until our hearts knew not which most to feel, delight or dread.

When she was dying, she said, to one who loved her,—

"Will you give me a beautiful blue dress?

And he said.—

"God is making a beautiful dress for you, my child."

So the lovely creature's spirit went to meet Angel's, and she was laid, meek and peaceful, in her coffin, and knew tears no more.

Then those who loved her, thought, "What shall we do with Angel's doll? no one should have it but Cherub."

So they took the doll, and laid it softly in Cherub's arms, in the coffin, and its red cheeks and bright eyes were pillowed near the pale, calm face of the child.

They rest together in a tranquil grave-yard, and evergreens grow around them.

THE FALCON.

# THE FALCON FAMILY.

THOSE diurnal birds of prey which can be trained for hunting are termed Nobiles, or Noble; and among them are almost all those which form the falcon or hawk tribe. They equal eagles in courage; and although they are inferior in size and strength, they are superior in docility, gentleness, and entire obedience to the commands of those who train them for use or amusement.

The beak of falcons is very strong, and much more curved than that of any other

(31)

bird of prey; it is also shorter, and has
a projection from each edge of the upper
part, like a sharply pointed tooth. The
wings are long, and end in a point on
one side; which shape obliges these
birds to fly in a slanting direction when
the weather is calm, and if they wish to
rise in a straight line, they are forced to
fly against the wind. They do not seek
dead prey, and pursue their game at full
speed, falling down upon it perpendicu-
larly with great swiftness. Old birds
differ much from the young in plumage,
and the colors are brown, white, black,
and gray, and occasionally a reddish tint;
the female is generally one-third larger
than the male; the eye-brows of both
project very much, which gives them a

very peculiar appearance, and their eyes are remarkably brilliant. The size varies from that of a large cock to a pigeon; the legs are blue or yellow, and there is a great variety of shape in the spots and bands formed by the feathers.

In consequence of falconry, or hawking, having been in former times a sport among all classes in northern nations, many curious laws were made about the practice of it, as at this day we find for shooting, fishing, or hunting with dogs; and a great deal of money was spent in keeping and training these birds. In those days it was only thought necessary for a nobleman to understand hawking, hunting, and exercise of arms; and he might, if he pleased, leave study and learning to those who were of a rank beneath his own, without being remarkable for his ignorance. There are many old portraits of noblemen and gentlemen, and even ladies, (for they used to join in the sport on horseback,) with falcons on their wrists; and King Harold was represented with a bird on his hand and a dog under his arm. The chief falconer was the fourth officer in rank at court, at the time when Wales had its own kings; but he was only allowed to take three draughts a day out of his drinking horn, for fear he should get tipsy and neglect his birds.

The expenses of falconry being so enormous, those who infringed the laws respecting it were often severely punished.

THE COMMON FALCON,

From a very old book we learn, that to
steal a hawk, or even its eggs when found
by chance, in the time of Edward II.,
subjected a person to imprisonment, and
to pay a sum of money. It was the
same in the time of Queen Elizabeth,
with the additions that the offender was
obliged to find some one who would answer for his good behaviour for seven
years; and if he could not procure any
one to do so, he was forced to remain in
prison for that period.

A thousand pounds are said to have
been given for a set of hawks, although
the birds were procured in England,
Wales, Scotland, and Ireland; these
large sums, therefore, must have been
paid for the trouble of training them.

Occasionally they were brought from Norway, and were then so much thought of, that they were esteemed fit for a sovereign. King John had two given to him as a bribe for allowing a man to trade in cheese.

Among the different kinds used in sport, the Perigrine falcon was reckoned the best, and is now the only one kept for the purpose in England, and that very rarely. Henry II. is said to have sent for some of them every year into Pembrokeshire. It however lives in most of the northern parts of the earth, and its flight is so rapid, that there are few countries which it does not visit.

The Gyr falcon is one of the largest of the tribe; its legs and beak are yellow, and it was formerly trained to catch cranes, herons, and wild geese. The Goshawk was also flown at the same prey, but more especially at pheasants and partridges. Among the smaller trained species was the Kestril, which nests in the holes of ruins, high towers, or clefts of rocks; its chief food is field-mice, and it is that hawk which we see remaining a long time in the air in one spot, fanning its wings and watching for its prey. The Hobby, also a small species, was taught to catch larks, and was thrown from the hand near their haunts, when the poor little creatures would crowd together and remain motionless from fear; a net was then thrown over them, and all were secured.

The Kite, the Sparrowhawk, the Hen-harrier, the Merlin, and the Buzzard, do not appear to have been used for sporting. The first builds its nests in large forests, and has a forked tail. It may be known in the air from all other birds by its smooth flight, for its wings scarcely seem to move, and it appears frequently to remain motionless for a time. There is an old saying, that when kites fly high it will be fair weather; and the famous Pliny, who lived in the last times of the ancient Romans, and wrote a great deal about birds, says that the invention of the rudder for steering boats and ships was taken from the motion of a kite's tail.

The Sparrowhawk is a great enemy to

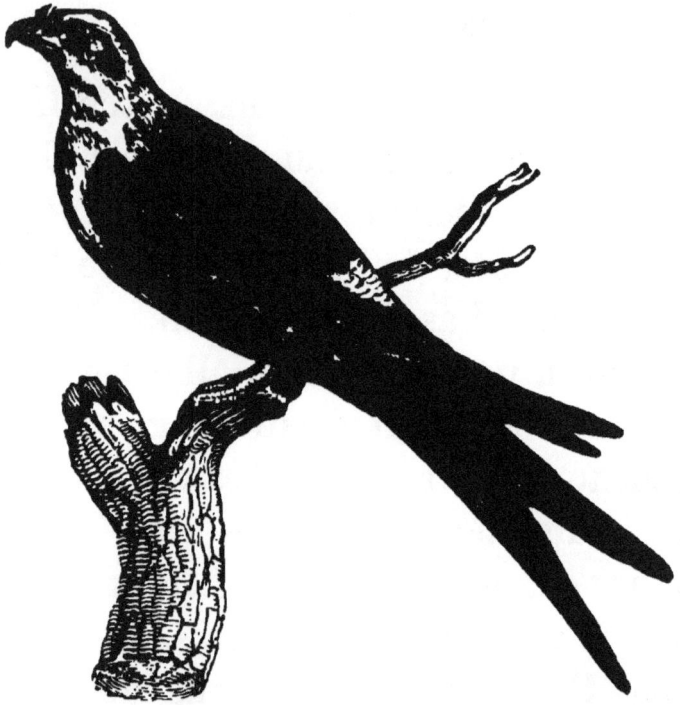

THE KITE.

pigeons and partridges; and it and the Hen-harrier are very destructive to poultry. When we hear a hen cackle, and see her cower down upon the ground, and anxiously cover all her chickens with her wings, we may be sure that one of these destroyers is in the neighborhood. The Merlin, although small, is a very courageous bird, flies low, and skims along the tops of the hedges in search of its prey; it kills partridges by one stroke upon the neck.

The Buzzards are much less active than other hawks, they eat frogs, lizards, mice, rabbits, birds, worms, and insects; and one of them, which frequents moors and marshy places, never soars into the air. It is a very voracious bird, and

kills many young ducks; its legs are
longer and more slender than those of
hawks in general, by which it is better
enabled to find its way through wet
places.

# THE WINDOW PANE AT NIGHT.

" Oh, what is the matter, my child!
Your looks are most awfully wild,—
    Why leave off your usual play?
Not noisy, for I heard not a sound,—
Now you throw down your doll on the
    ground,—
    Do listen, my Maud, and obey.

" Here's plenty of light—as you see,
Though you'd play in the dark far from
    me,
    Behind the red curtain you ran,

But now you run frightened about,
Of the reason you leave me in doubt;
   Pray tell me the cause—if you can?"

"Papa, at the window I saw!—"
"An owl, I suppose, or jackdaw."
   "Oh, no, but a robber, I'm sure!
She stared at me full in the face!"
"What, one of the poor gipsy race?"—
   "Why, no, I can't say she look'd
     *poor*.

"Her face is as rosy as mine;
Her eyes are bright blue—and they
     shine,
   But yet she began to look pale,
And opening her mouth as if crying,
I felt as if *I*, too, was dying!"
   "Well, this is a wondrous tale!"

"O cruel papa, how you laugh!
As if 'twere a cow or a calf,
   That really *is* your belief.
Papa might, I think, believe *me*—
Do go to the window and see,
     Then send out and catch the young
       thief!"

He took little Maud in his arms,
And said "These are foolish alarms,
   The pretty '*young thief*' I have caught!
Come now to the window with me,
And then you will speedily see
   The wonder the window-glass wrought."

Quickly holding her up to the pane,
She saw the same face come again!
   And there was papa's face also!

Convinced now, she bashfully smiled,
The glass showed a sweet smiling child!
　　"Then this is the case,
　　　*I saw my own face!*" .
Which truth little Maud was most
　　happy to know.

NEW AND ATTRACTIVE

# JUVENILE BOOKS.

BOSTON:

CROSBY & AINSWORTH.

NEW YORK: OLIVER S. FELT.

1866.

# Popular Juveniles.

---

ARABIAN NIGHTS' ENTERTAINMENTS. 12mo, muslin . . . .
   do.        do.        do.                do.         muslin, gilt . . .

ANYTHING FOR SPORT. By the author of "I Will be a Gentleman,"
   &c. 18mo. . . . . . . . . . . . .

A NEW FLOWER FOR CHILDREN. By L. MARIA CHILD. Illustrated . . . . . . . . . . . . .

ARBELL'S SCHOOL DAYS. By JANE WINNARD HOOPER. Illustrated .

A STRIKE FOR FREEDOM; or, Law and Order. By the author of
   " I Will be a Gentleman." &c. 18mo . . . . . . .

I WILL BE A SAILOR. By Mrs. L. C. TUTHILL . . . .

THE WILD MAN OF THE WEST. By R. M. BALLANTYNE. Illustrated. 16mo . . . . . . . . . . . .

THE RED ERIC; or, the Whaler's Last Cruise. By R. M. BALLANTYNE. Illustrated. 16mo . . . . . . . . . . .

DICK RODNEY; or, Adventures of an Eton Boy. By the author of "Jack
   Manly," &c. Illustrated. 16mo . . . . . . .

TALES FROM GENESIS. By Rev. WM. M. THAYER. author of "The Poor
   Boy and Merchant Prince," "The Bobbin Boy," &c. Illustrated. 2 vols. 16mo

AUDUBON, THE NATURALIST OF THE NEW WORLD;
   his Adventures and Discoveries. By Mrs. HORACE ST. JOHN. Illustrated .

A WILL AND A WAY. Tales from the German. Six colored illustrations . . . . . . . . . . .

BELLE AND LILLY; or, The Golden Rule. A Story for Girls. By a
   New Pen. With colored illustrations . . . . . .

BEARS OF AUGUSTUSBURG; an Episode in Saxon History. With six
   colored engravings printed in oil colors. 16mo. cloth . . . .

BOY OF MOUNT RHIGI. By Miss C. M. SEDGWICK. . . . .

BEAR-HUNTERS OF THE ROCKY MOUNTAINS. By ANNE
   BOWMAN. With illustrations . . . . . . . .

**BOARDING - SCHOOL GIRL.** By the author of "I Will be a Gentleman," &c. . . . . . . . . . . . . .

**BOY OF SPIRIT.** By Miss Tuthill . . . . . . . .

**CANADIAN CRUSOES.** A Tale of the Plains. By Catherine Parr Traill. Edited by her sister, Agnes Strickland. Illustrated

**CHILDREN'S FRIEND.** From the French of M. Berquin. With thirty illustrations . . . . . . . . . .

**COUSIN HATTY'S HYMNS AND TWILIGHT STORIES.** With numerous engravings. Square 16mo . . . . .

**CHILDHOOD OF MARY LEESON.** By Mary Howitt. 18mo . .

**CHILDREN'S TRIALS;** or, The Little Rope Dancers, and other Tales. With six beautiful engravings, printed in oil colors . . . .

**CHILDREN'S YEAR.** By Mary Howitt. Illustrated . . . .

**DOG CRUSOE.** By R. M. Ballantyne, author of "Hudson's Bay," &c. . .

**ELLEN STANLEY, AND OTHER STORIES** . . . .

**FLORENCE ERWIN'S THREE HOMES.** A Tale of North and South . . . . . . . . . . . . .

**FLOWERS FOR CHILDREN.** By L. Maria Child . . . .

**FANNY GRAY.** Comprising a History of her Life in a series of six beautiful Figures printed in oil colors. In a neat box . . . . .

**FRANK WILDMAN'S ADVENTURES.** By Frederick Gerstaecker. Illustrated with eight crayon drawings in oil colors. 12mo, cloth, gilt, . .

**GORILLA-HUNTERS.** A Tale of the Woods of Africa. By R. M. Ballantyne. Illustrated . . . . . . . . .

**GRIMM'S POPULAR TALES AND HOUSEHOLD STORIES.** Newly translated, with nearly 200 illustrations by Edward H. Wehnert. In 2 vols.

| do. | do. | do. | do. | 1 vol. 12mo |
| do. | do. | do. | do. | muslin, gilt |

**HARRY AND AGGIE;** or, The Ride. A new and beautiful series of Figures printed in colors. In a neat box . . . . . . .

**HURRAH FOR THE HOLIDAYS!** With six colored illustrations .

**HURRAH FOR NEW ENGLAND!**

**HYMNS, SONGS, AND FABLES.** By Mrs. Follen . . . .

**I WILL BE A SOLDIER.** By Mrs. Tuthill. Illustrated. 16mo, cloth

**I WILL BE A GENTLEMAN.** By Mrs. Tuthill. 18mo, cloth . .

**I WILL BE A LADY.** A Book for Girls. By Mrs. Tuthill . . .

**JOHN CHINAMAN;** or, Adventures in Flowery Land. By William Dalton. 16mo, Illustrated. Cloth . . . . . . . . .

KANGAROO-HUNTERS; or, Adventures in the Bush. By ANNE BOWMAN. Illustrated . . . . . . . . . . . . .

LEILA; or, The Island. By ANN FRASER TYTLER. With engravings . .

LEILA IN ENGLAND. A continuation of "Leila; or, The Island." Illustrated . . . . . . . . . . .

LEILA AT HOME. A continuation of "Leila in England." Illustrated .

LITTLE FRANKIE STORIES. By Mrs. MADELINE LESLIE. Illustrated by Billings. Price, single vol. 25 cents. Set, six vols. . . .

LIFE OF LAFAYETTE. For Children. By E. CECIL. With colored engravings . . . . . . . . . . . .

LAND OF THE SUN; or, What Kate and Willie saw in Cuba. By CORNELIA H. JENKS. Illustrated . . . . . . . .

LIFE OF WASHINGTON. For Children. By E. CECIL. With colored engravings. 16mo . . . . . . . . .

MARY AND FLORENCE; or, Grave and Gay. By ANN FRASER TYTLER, author of the "Leila Books." Illustrated . . . . .

MARY AND FLORENCE AT SIXTEEN. By ANN FRASER TYTLER. Illustrated . . . . . . . . . . .

MOLLY AND KITTY; with other Tales. With six beautiful engravings printed in oil colors . . . . . . . . .

MANY A LITTLE MAKES A MICKLE. Tales translated from the German. With six colored plates . . . . . .

MISS EDGEWORTH'S EARLY LESSONS. By Miss MARIA EDGEWORTH. 5 vols. cloth . . . . . . . . .

MARK SEAWORTH; a Tale of the Indian Ocean. By WM. H. G. KINGSTON, Esq. Illustrated . . . . . . . . .

MERRY TALES FOR LITTLE FOLKS. Illustrated . . .

MOTHER'S TRUE STORIES. A New Book of Bible Stories. With six engravings printed in oil colors. Square 16mo . . . .

NORVA; A TALE OF THE ROMAN EMPIRE. With other Stories. By EMILE SOUVESTRE, author of "The Attic Philosopher in Paris," &c. With engravings . . . . . . . . .

NANNIE'S JEWEL CASE; or, True Stones and False. With six colored illustrations . . . , . . . . .

ONWARD! RIGHT ONWARD! By. Mrs. TUTHILL . . . .

PEARLS, AND OTHER TALES. With six colored illustrations . .

POPULAR LEGENDS OF BRITTANY. From a German Translation by HEINRICH BODE. With 16 beautiful engravings. Colored . . .

PICTURES OF COMICAL PEOPLE, with Stories about them. For Children of all ages. With numerous illustrations from designs by Granville, Orr, and others . . . . . . . . . . .

**THE FIRESIDE; OR, HINTS ON HOME EDUCATION.** By A. B. Muzzey, author of "The Young Maiden," "The Young Man's Friend," &c. 16mo, cloth, gilt . . . . . . . . . .

**MABEL VAUGHAN.** By the author of the "Lamplighter." 1 vol. 12mo .

**TUNE-BOOK FOR THE CONGREGATION.** A Collection of Tunes for use in Societies, and for Vestry and Conference Meetings. Cloth . . .

**THE ECLIPSE OF FAITH;** or, a Visit to a Religious Sceptic. By Henry Rogers, author of "Reason and Faith," and "Miscellaneous." 12mo, cloth .

**A DEFENCE OF "THE ECLIPSE OF FAITH."** By its Author. Being a Rejoinder to Prof. Newman's "Reply." Also the "Reply" by Prof. Newman. 1 vol. 12mo, cloth . . . . . . . . .

**THE STARS AND THE EARTH;** or, Thoughts upon Space, Time, and Eternity. 18mo, flex. cloth . . . . . . . .

**HYPATIA;** or, New Foes with an Old Face. By C. M. Kingsley, author of "Yeast," "Alton Locke," &c. 1 vol. 12mo . . . . . .

**THE TEACHER'S ASSISTANT;** or, Hints and Methods in School Discipline and Instruction. By Charles Northend, A.M. 12mo. . . . .

**WARE'S FORMATION OF CHRISTIAN CHARACTER, AND SEQUEL.** 16mo, bevelled red edges . . . . . . .

**CHANNING'S SELF-CULTURE, AND LECTURES TO THE LABORING CLASSES.** 16mo, bevelled red edges . . . . .

**DEXTER'S SERMONS.** Twelve Discourses. By Henry Martin Dexter. With Portrait. 8vo, cloth . . . . . . . . .

**STREET THOUGHTS.** By Rev. H. M. Dexter, Pastor of the Pine-street Church, Boston. With illustrations by Billings. 16mo, cloth . . .

**HOME COOKERY.** A Collection of Tried Receipts, both Foreign and Domestic. By Mrs. J. Chadwick. 12mo, half bound . . . . . .

**DUELS AND DUELLING.** Alphabetically arranged. With an Historical Essay. By Lorenzo Sabine. 12mo . . . . . . . .

**I'VE BEEN THINKING.** By A. S. Roe . . . . . . .

**HOW COULD HE HELP IT?** By A. S. Roe . . . . .

**STAR AND CLOUD.** By A. S. Roe . . . . . . . .

**TO LOVE AND TO BE LOVED.** By A. S. Roe . . . . .

**TRUE TO THE LAST.** By A. S. Roe . . . . . . .

**LONG LOOK AHEAD.** By A. S. Roe . . . . . . .

**THE NORTH AMERICAN REVIEW.** Issued in numbers quarterly Per annum . . . . . . . . . . .

**THE MARRIAGE OFFERING.** A Compilation of Prose and Poetry. By A. A. LIVERMORE. With two engravings on steel by Andrews, from designs by Billings. Cloth, gilt . . . . . . . . . . . . . .

do.    do.    do.    do.    cloth, extra, gilt . . . . . .

**PASTOR'S WEDDING GIFT.** By Rev. WILLIAM M. THAYER. 16mo, muslin, gilt, extra . . . . . . . . . . . . .

**TUPPER'S PROVERBIAL PHILOSOPHY.** 12mo, muslin . .

do.    do.    do.    muslin, gilt, extra . . . .

do    do.    do.    morocco, do. . . . . . .

**GLEANINGS FROM THE POETS.** By Mrs. LOWELL. 12mo, muslin

do.    do.    do.    muslin, gilt, extra . . . . .

do.    do.    do.    morocco do. . . . . .

**OUR FAVORITE POETS.** Illustrated with engravings. 1 vol. 12mo, cloth

do.    do.    do.    full gilt . . . . . . .

**HISTORY OF THE UNITED STATES.** By MURRAY. Illustrated. 1 vol. 8vo, muslin . . . . . . . . . . . . .

do.    do.    do.    do.    sheep . . . .

**LIBRARY OF NATURAL HISTORY.** By GOULD. 400 engravings. 1 vol. 8vo, muslin . . . . . . . . . . . .

do.    do.    do.    do.    sheep . . . .

**CHRISTIAN BELIEVING AND LIVING.** A Series of Discourses by Rev. FREDERICK D. HUNTINGTON, D.D. 12mo . . . . . . .

**SERMONS FOR THE PEOPLE.** By Rev. F. D. HUNTINGTON, D.D. 12mo, cloth . . . . . . . . . . . . . .

**HOME AND COLLEGE.** By Rev. F. D. HUNTINGTON, D.D. 16mo . .

**JACK IN THE FORECASTLE.** By Capt. JOHN S. SLEEPER. Eight engravings. 12mo, cloth . . . . . . . . . . .

**LIFE AND RELIGION OF THE HINDOOS.** With a Sketch of my Life and Experience. By JOGUTH CHUNDER GANGOOLY. 16mo, cloth .

**MARION GRAHAM;** or, Higher than Happiness. A Novel. By the author of "Light on the Dark River." Cloth . . . . . . . .

**RELIGIOUS LECTURES ON THE PECULIAR PHENOMENA IN THE FOUR SEASONS.** By EDWARD HITCHCOCK, LL.D. 16 mo, cloth . . . . . . . . . . . . . .

**THE ADVENTURES OF JAMES CAPEN ADAMS.** Ilustrated by 12 engravings. 12mo, cloth . . . . . . . . .

**THOUGHTS TO HELP AND TO CHEER.** Comprising a Selection from Scripture, a Meditation, and a Poetical Extract for each day in the year. 24mo, blue and gold . . . . . . . . . . .

**WELL BEGUN IS HALF DONE; AND, THE YOUNG ARTIST.** With six fine illustrations printed in oil colors . . . . .

**WILD SPORTS IN THE FAR WEST.** By FREDERICK GERSTAECKER. Illustrated with eight crayon drawings in oil colors. 12mo, gilt, cloth . . . .

**YOUNG ISLANDERS; or, The School-boy Crusoes. A Tale of the Last Century.** By JEFFREYS TAYLOR. Cloth . . . . . . . . . .

---

# Miscellaneous.

**ARABIAN NIGHTS' ENTERTAINMENTS.** Illustrated, muslin .
do.   do.   do.   muslin, gilt, extra .
do.   do.   do.   morocco, do. .

**NOBLE DEEDS OF WOMEN.** By Miss STARLING. 12mo, muslin .
do.   do.   do.   do.   muslin, gilt, extra . . .
do.   do.   do.   do.   morocco, do. . . . .

**BANCROFT'S LIFE OF GEORGE WASHINGTON.** With illustrations. 12mo, muslin . . . . . .
do.   do.   do.   do   muslin, gilt, extra .

**LIFE AND CAMPAIGNS OF NAPOLEON BONAPARTE.** With illustrations. 12mo, muslin . . . . . . . .
do.   do.   muslin, gilt, extra . . . . . .

**FROST'S LIVES OF THE PRESIDENTS OF THE UNITED STATES.** With Portraits. 12mo, muslin . . . . . .
do.   do.   muslin, gilt, extra . . . .

**YOUNG LADY'S OFFERING.** Bv Mrs. SIGOURNEY. 12mo, muslin .
do.   do.   do.   muslin, gilt, extra . . . .
do.   do.   do.   morocco, do. . . . .

**YOUNG MAN'S OFFERING.** By Professor ANDREWS. 12mo, muslin .
do.   do.   do.   muslin, gilt . . . .
do.   do.   do.   morocco . . . . .

**FLORA'S LEXICON.** An Interpretation of Languages of Flowers. Colored illustrations.   muslin . . . . . .
do.   do.   muslin, gilt, extra . . . . .
do.   do.   morocco . . . . . .

**TALES FROM SHAKSPEARE.** By CHARLES LAMB. 12mo, muslin .
do,   do.   do.   muslin, gilt, extra . . . . .
do.   do.   do.   morocco, do. . . . .
**THE YOUNG MAIDEN.** By A. B. MUZZEY. With two engravings on steel by Schoff, designed by Billings. 16mo, cloth, gilt . . . . .
do.   do.   do.   cloth, extra, gilt edges . . . .

**POPULAR TALES.** By Madame Guizot. Translated 'from the French. With six colored engravings . . . . . . . .

**PETER THE WHALER.** By Wm. H. G. Kingston, Esq. Illustrated .

**PLAYMATE.** A very beautiful book, with nearly 200 engravings. Square 16mo., gilt, cloth . . . . . . . . . .
do.      do.      do.      do.      extra .

**ROBINSON CRUSOE.** By De Foe. Square 16mo. Illustrated, muslin .

**ROBIN HOOD AND HIS MERRY FORESTERS.** By Stephen Percy. Illustrated . . . . . . . . .

**ROBIN-NEST STORIES.** By Mrs. Madeline Leslie. Illustrated by Billings. Price 25 cents, single volume. Set, six vols..

**ROUND THE WORLD.** A Tale for Boys. By W. H. G. Kingston. With illustrations. 16mo, cloth, gilt . . . . . . . .

**SICKNESS AND HEALTH OF THE PEOPLE OF BLEA-BURN.** 18mo, gilt, cloth . . . . . . .

**SEED-TIME AND HARVEST.** By Trauermantel. With six colored illustrations . . . . . . . . .

**STORIES ABOUT THE INSTINCTS OF ANIMALS, THEIR CHARACTERS AND HABITS.** By Thomas Bingley. Illustrated .

**STORIES AND LEGENDS FROM MANY LANDS.** Illustrated . . . . . . . . .

**SWISS FAMILY ROBINSON;** or, The Adventures of a Father, Mother, and Four Sons, in a Desert Island. The general progress of the story furnishes a clear illustration of the first principles of Natural History, and many branches of science which most immediately apply to the business of life. Complete .

**STORIES OF THE CANADIAN FOREST;** or, Little Mary and her Nurse. By Mrs. Traill (sister of Agnes Strickland). Illustrated . . .

**SALT WATER;** or, The Sea Life and Adventures of Neil D'Arcy, the Midshipman. By Wm. H. G. Kingston, Esq. Illustrated by Anelay . . . .

**TALES FROM THE HISTORY OF THE SAXONS.** By Emily Taylor. Illustrated . . . . . . . . .

**TITANIA: TALES AND LEGENDS.** Six colored illustrations .

**THE WONDERFUL MIRROR.** With colored engravings. 16mo, cloth

**THE WIND SPIRIT AND THE RAIN GODDESS.** With nearly 100 beautiful colored engravings . . . . . .

**TALES WORTH TELLING;** or, a Traveller's Adventures by Sea and Land. Illustrated with 133 engravings . . . . . .

**WHEN ARE WE HAPPIEST?** By the author of "The Boy of Spirit," &c. . . . . . . . . . .

# Juvenile Libraries.

EACH IN A NEAT BOX, AND EVERY VOLUME FULLY ILLUSTRATED.

**DOG CRUSOE SERIES.** By R. M. Ballantyne, Kingston, Bowman, and others. 6 vols. 16mo, cloth
The Gorilla-hunters.
Audubon.
Round the World.
The Bear-hunters.
Dog Crusoe.
John Chinaman.

**SALT-WATER TALES.** By Wm. H. G. Kingston. 4 vols.
The Young Islanders.
Peter the Whaler.
Mark Seaworth.
Salt Water.

**MOUNT-VERNON JUVENILES.** 6 vols.
Life of Washington.
Love of Country.
Bears of Augustusburg.
Life of Lafayette.
Legends of Brittany.
Hurrah for the Holidays!

**MERRY TALES AND STORIES FOR YOUNG FOLKS.** 6 vols.
Stories of the Canadian Forest.
Pictures of Comical People.
Canadian Crusoes.
Tales of the Saxons.
The Kangaroo-hunters.
Merry Tales.

**THE MOLLY AND KITTY JUVENILES.** 6 vols.
Molly and Kitty.
Children's Trials.
Tales and Legends.
Seedtime and Harvest.
Belle and Lily.
Holly and Mistletoe.

**THE LEILA BOOKS.** By Ann Fraser Tytler. 5 vols.
Leila at Home.
Leila in England.
Leila; or, The Island.
Mary and Florence.
Mary and Florence at Sixteen.

**THE ROBIN-NEST STORIES.** By Mrs. Madeline Leslie. 6 vols.
The Robins' Nest.
Little Robins Learning to Fly.
Little Robins' Friends.
Little Robins in the Nest.
Little Robins in Trouble.
Little Robins' Love to one another.

**LITTLE FRANKIE STORIES.** By Mrs. Madeline Leslie. 6 vols.
Little Frankie and his Mother.
Little Frankie and his Father.
Little Frankie at his Plays.
Little Frankie and his Cousin.
Little Frankie on a Journey.
Little Frankie at School.

**TALES AND STORIES WORTH TELLING.** 4 vols.
Robin Hood.
Mother's True Stories.
Bingley's Instincts of Animals.
Tales Worth Telling.

**THE JEWEL CASE.** 6 vols.
The Pearls.
Guizot's Popular Tales.
Well Begun is Half Done.
Many a Little makes a Mickle.
A Will and a Way.
Nannie's Jewel Case.

**EDGEWORTH'S EARLY LESSONS.** 5 vols. . . . . .

Frank.
Sequel to Frank.
Rosamond.
Harry and Lucy.
Harry and Lucy, concluded.

**MRS. TUTHILL'S JUVENILE LIBRARY.** 14 vols. . .

I will be a Gentleman.
I will be a Lady.
Happy Days, and the Warning.
A Strike for Freedom.
Onward! Right Onward!
The Sickness and Health of the People of Bleaburn.
The Boarding-school Girl.

The Boy of Spirit.
When are we Happiest?
Hurrah for New England!
The Childhood of Mary Leeson.
Ellen Stanley, and other Stories.
Anything for Sport.
Keeper's Travels in Search of his Master.

**YOUNG PEOPLE'S LIBRARY.** 12 vols. . . . . . .

Alphabet of Birds.
Alphabet of Animals.
Young Rabbit-fancier.
Annie and the Elves.
Stories and Legends.
The Boa Constrictor.

Johnny and Maggie.
The Princess Unca.
Lucy's Canary.
Christmas Eve.
Rose Tremain.
Just in Time.

**UNCLE SAM'S LIBRARY FOR THE BOYS AND GIRLS.**

The Christmas Eve.
George and his Dog.
Stories and Legends.

The Picture Alphabets.
All for the Best.
The Eskdale Herdboy.

**SIX PLEASANT COMPANIONS FOR SPARE HOURS.** Embellished with nearly 200 engravings. Square 16mo, fancy cloth, gilt . .

Little Freddy and his Fiddle.
Little Lizzie and the Fairies.
The Road to Fortune.

Saddler Muller's Wendell.
Tony, the Sleepless.
Finikin and his Gold Pippins.

**BOUQUETS FOR CHILDREN.** Collected by L. MARIA CHILD, MARY Howitt, and others. 5 vols. . . . . . . . . .

New Flower for Children.
Flowers for Children.
Arbell's School-days,
The Children's Year.
Berquin's Children's Friend.

**YOUTHS' PICTORIAL LIBRARY.** With over 500 illustrations. 12 vols., 16mo, paper covers, per set . . . . . . . .
do. do. muslin, gilt, do. . . . . . . .

Poems for Little Folks.
Tales of the Great and Brave.
Stories of Animals.
Christmas Stories.
Stories of Natural History.
Rabbit's Bride, and other Stories.

Tales of Adventure.
Stories of Foreign Countries.
Casper's Adventure.
Fairy Stories.
Fables in Verse.
History of Birds.

9 783744 686198